# THE ROWMAN & LITTLEFIELD GUIDE TO WRITING WITH SOURCES

# THE ROWMAN & LITTLEFIELD GUIDE TO WRITING WITH SOURCES

## THIRD EDITION

JAMES P. DAVIS

**ROWMAN & LITTLEFIELD PUBLISHERS, INC.**
Lanham • Boulder • New York • Toronto • Plymouth, UK

# ROWMAN & LITTLEFIELD PUBLISHERS, INC.

Published in the United States of America
by Rowman & Littlefield Publishers, Inc.
A wholly owned subsidary of The Rowman & Littlefield Publishing Group, Inc.
4501 Forbes Boulevard, Suite 200, Lanham, MD 20706
www.rowmanlittlefield.com

Estover Road, Plymouth PL6 7PY, United Kingdom

British Library Cataloguing in Publication Information Available

**Library of Congress Cataloging-in-Publication Data**

Davis, James P., 1954–
  The Rowman & Littlefield guide to writing with sources / James P. Davis. — 3rd
ed.
     p. cm.
  Includes bibliographical references.
  ISBN-13: 978-0-7425-5413-9 (pbk. : alk. paper)
  ISBN-10: 0-7425-5413-9 (pbk. : alk. paper)
  1. English language—Rhetoric—Handbooks, manuals, etc. 2. Research—Method-
ology—Handbooks, manuals, etc. 3. Report writing—Handbooks, manuals, etc.  I.
Title. II. Title: Rowman and Littlefield guide to writing with sources. III. Title:
Guide to writing with sources.
  PE1478.D37 2007
  808'.0042072—dc22

                              2006031735

Printed in the United States of America

♾ ™ The paper used in this publication meets the minimum requirements of
American National Standard for Information Sciences—Permanence of Paper
for Printed Library Materials, ANSI/NISO Z39.48-1992.
Manufactured in the United States of America.

# CONTENTS

# "TRUTHINESS" AND THE CHALLENGES OF ACADEMIC WRITING

It's getting too difficult to find nonfiction. Perhaps that's a strange claim when nonfiction books and memoirs are enjoying robust sales. Nonfiction documentary films are getting widespread release at neighborhood cine-plexes, and nothing boosts a movie's popularity quite like the claim that it's "based on a real story" or "inspired by real events." News programs are pro-liferating throughout network and cable television, and some of the most pop-ular prime-time shows are "reality-based." The market reveals that the public has an appetite for truth, reality, nonfiction—whatever we choose to call it. Yet much of what passes for truth is clearly something else—doublespeak, propa-ganda, plagiarism, advertising, public relations, fraud, spin—what Comedy Central's Stephen Colbert calls "truthiness," a claim or position expressed with seeming certainty that is based not on evidence but on little more than the desire for it to be true.

The media are drawing attention to misrepresentations of information, as is evident in the catch phrases and issues of national news stories. We read that the Iraq War was based on "faulty intelligence." We're told there's a "cul-ture of corruption" in Washington. Authors and political figures accuse each other of "rewriting history." With accusations of bribery, fraud, intelligence leaks, election rigging—these are times when conspiracy theories are abun-dant, when people are highly skeptical of what they're told, when they pre-sume that a degree of deceit is at work in virtually everything they read or watch. Magazines, critics claim, are under the corporate thumb of advertisers who demand "complimentary copy" and "advertorials" before they provide the essential funding for the publications. Newspapers, we're told, offer perspectives biased by the Left or by the Right. Such esteemed newspapers as *The New York Times*, *The Atlanta Journal-Constitution*, *USA Today*, and *The Los Angeles Times* have recently dismissed plagiarists and issued apologies. Internationally acclaimed scientists have fabricated data about such vital topics as stem cell research and cold nuclear fusion. *USA Today* claims, "The Internet is becoming a cesspool of plagiarism" (Jones 3B). James Frey's best-selling, allegedly autobiographical memoir *A Million Little Pieces* fooled Oprah Winfrey and energized debate about how true nonfiction needs to be. Lawsuits over instances of plagiarism in popular music and best-selling books are commonplace. Broadcast and cable news agencies offer programming so attuned to the sensational and the safe that many viewers prefer to view self-described "fake news" programs (like *The Daily Show* and *The Colbert Report*). Syndicated columnist Frank Rich argues that our obsession with "fictional nonfiction" has moved beyond the reality TV shows whose dialogue is scripted in advance by teams of writers: "What's remarkable is how much fictionalization plays a role in almost every national debate." For 2005, the American Dialect Society chose Colbert's "truthiness" as Word of the Year.

We hope that colleges and universities are havens of clarity, integrity, and critical thinking—where standards of reasonable argumentation and ethics guide communities of teachers and students as they test ideas and learn to reach valid conclusions. Of course, colleges have that potential and sometimes attain it. But they haven't been immune to sloppiness and deceit, as we're reminded whenever we read of a college president, dean, or professor who has been accused of plagiarism. In a graduate program at one large university, more than three dozen current and former students have been accused of plagiarizing in their master's theses (Gray). According to a survey of 50,000 students on over 60 campuses, 70 percent of students admit to having cheated, and half confess to "one or more instances of serious cheating on written assignments" (Campbell). Called a "plague" of plagiarism, this widespread academic dishonesty has been blamed on such things as the ease of cutting and pasting from the Internet or even on habits of intellectual theft encouraged by free music downloading on sites like Napster. It's likely that the continual invention of new technologies and types of sources has left students (and even some of their teachers) confused about how to assess, select, and use both published and electronic information.

Given the challenges posed by abundant material of questionable reliability, it's doubly important that you learn how to make the complex choices involved when you're reading, researching, and writing. Reading with a critical eye involves essential intellectual skills, as you assess the relationship of the information you have found to your project, evaluate its credibility and relevance, select the best use of the material, represent it accurately and fairly, and fully and coherently integrate it into your project. You must also acknowledge and cite the sources you have used in a methodical and clear way. Whether you quote them or paraphrase the information you have found; whether they are published books, unsigned articles, or documents found on the Internet; and whether your project is a formal report, a personal essay, or an oral report in a seminar, you must clearly signal that you have employed these resources and learn to cite them in ways that are ethical, precise, rhetorically effective, and consistent with practices established for the field in which you are writing. Learning to read critically and to write responsibly is crucial—not merely to staying out of trouble but to making sense of one's position during a time of truthiness. Consistently practicing the skills discussed in this book will help you to detect misuse of information by others and to write with more confidence and clearer purpose yourself.

## DECISIONS TO MAKE

When you wish to use some information you've found or to quote a viewpoint that is expressed in some source, you need to make a number of decisions.

- Do you need to acknowledge the source of your information?
- Should you paraphrase or quote the material?
- If quoting, how much of the passage should you reproduce in your paper?
- How should you introduce and present the material?

- How should you make the transition to the quoted material and then back to your own prose so that your readers will always understand the status of the words they are reading?
- How should you cite electronic and Internet sources?

This book will help you to answer these questions.


## PLAGIARISM

The writing skills involved in using quotations or information from sources are basic ones that you must employ in all of your writing. Your ability to use sources ethically and clearly is crucial to your success in every course, in any major you pursue, in whatever profession you choose. Yet college students often lack these basic skills. The purpose of this book is to enable you to incorporate quoted or paraphrased material into your writing in ways that credit the sources you consult for wording or ideas that are not your own and that will permit your audience to comprehend your ideas and to have confidence in your authority as a writer. Mastering the skills discussed here will broaden your options as you write, increase your confidence as a student, and empower you to write with clarity and authority. Neglecting these skills will cripple your abilities to communicate and, worse, in some cases, render you vulnerable to charges of academic dishonesty.

Very few students plan to cheat when they begin a course or when they begin a specific project. Most cases of academic dishonesty arise from poor planning, procrastination, carelessness, or intrusions of stress into students' lives that they haven't learned to manage. As a deadline approaches, they might be tempted to lift ideas or phrases from someone else's work. Or, in a rush to complete a project, they allow themselves to take such sloppy notes that they can no longer tell what is their phrasing or what is someone else's or which source might have provided something that is scrawled in their notebook. In an English class, they might feel they can use unacknowledged ideas from *Cliff's* notes or Sparknotes.com. Students usually realize that these are such undistinguished study guides that they don't want to disclose they've consulted them—but some of the wording or an occasional idea might seem too good not to use in an essay. Even if students don't think they are doing anything wrong, even if the idea or phrase trickled into their work through carelessness or haste, these violations are taken as seriously as if students copied someone else's lab report or put their name on an essay written by someone else. You shouldn't consult a source that you would be ashamed to cite. If you ever have a question about the way you are completing an assignment, ask your professor or lab assistant how to proceed. For example, although most instructors will not allow you to submit an essay written during a prior semester for a different class, it might be possible to combine two projects from different classes into one—but only if both professors are fully aware of and approve of what you're doing.

## DOONESBURY                    BY GARRY TRUDEAU

The Web has produced its own set of temptations to students. It might not seem like cheating when all one has to do is point and click to find some ready-made phrasing, without even needing to transcribe it. Students might genuinely believe, if they find some information or phrasing on more than one website, that it must be common knowledge or public property—forgetting that the websites themselves might have plagiarized from each other or some third source. But using any idea or information that is not common knowledge without carefully and properly acknowledging that you've done so is a form of serious academic dishonesty that—students are often surprised to learn—instructors detect easily. Instructors are familiar with the capabilities of most students and sensitive to features of individual students' writing styles. They are also familiar with the published work in their fields, well trained to recognize the contributions and stylistic habits of professional writers. A variety of specialized search engines and online services enable instructors to locate the original sources of wording and ideas stolen from published and electronic sources, often more quickly than the student was able to find it in the first place.

Plagiarism has never been so easy—but it has never been so easy to detect. No one enjoys being suspicious, and no task is more abhorrent to an instructor than confronting a dishonest or careless student and proceeding with judicial action. It is far more satisfying to work with students to train them to use sources responsibly before questions of their integrity arise. You must do your part to make certain that you understand this material and apply it whenever you write a paper. Don't let the fear of misusing quoted material dissuade you from doing research. Instead, master the skills of quoting and paraphrasing responsibly, confident that, when you do so, you will gain a powerful and indispensable skill.

## POPULAR STYLE MANUALS

Different disciplines follow different conventions for citing sources used in a project. Students might view these differences as unimportant, as if the rules are arbitrary or result from instructor preference. But formats for citing materials are not random. They have been designed by professional organizations to present citations in systematic ways that reflect the priorities and core values of that field. A book or pamphlet that presents a specific format is called a style manual. If an instructor has not specified which style manual to follow, it is a student's responsibility to ask which one to use and to follow its guidelines for formatting and printing the document and, most important, for how to arrange footnotes, endnotes, and a list of works cited. Most style manuals are available in your college or public library, and many are online. It's a good idea, once you have declared a major or begun graduate work within a particular field, to purchase a current copy of the style manual for that field. Some commonly used style manuals include the following:

1. Modern Language Association's *MLA Handbook for Writers of Research Papers*, for English and modern languages
2. Turabian's *Manual for Writers of Term Papers, Theses, and Dissertations*, for history and other humanities (based on the *Chicago Manual of Style*)
3. *Scientific Style and Format*, published by the Council of Science Editors (CSE), for biological sciences
4. *Publication Manual of the American Psychological Association* (APA) for psychology
5. *Handbook for Authors*, published by the American Chemical Society, for chemistry
6. *Style Manual for Political Science*, published by the American Political Science Association (APSA), for political science

This book does not present comprehensive citation formats for all fields. Because my discipline is English, my own citations will follow the format presented in the *MLA Handbook*. Whatever style manual you use for a particular course or paper, remember that the purpose of all of them is threefold:

1. To help you establish your authority and provide documentation for your claims in a systematic way
2. To help you provide your readers with all of the information they need to find your original sources and verify your claims about them
3. To provide a system for briefly identifying a source in your text with minimum textual clutter in ways that clearly refer to the fully cited work in a list at the end

## ELEMENTS REQUIRED IN A CITATION

Before you begin to gather information and take notes for a project, you need to know what sorts of information about the source you need to cite it properly—both in your list of works cited and in those portions of your text where you have used it.

If you are taking information from a book, all style sheets demand that you include in the final list:

- author
- title
- volume number (if a multivolume work)
- date of publication
- place of publication
- publisher
- page number(s)

Within your text itself, you may need to provide only the author's last name and a page number (or, for some disciplines, a year of publication). If you have used only one work by that author, it will be clear to which work in the list the name refers.

For articles, your works cited list must include:

- author
- title of the article
- title of the journal or magazine
- volume and issue numbers
- date
- page number(s)

As you do with books, in your text itself you should keep your information about a source as brief as you can, providing just enough information to enable your reader to identify the full citation in your list at the end. You refer to the full citation with the author's name (if known) or with an abbreviated title of the article (if the author is not known), and the page number.

Internet sources may or may not name their authors, and they won't have conventional page numbers. While you still have the source before you, you might need to go the home page or follow some other link to find out when the site was most recently revised and to find out the name of the author or sponsoring organization. If a website does not indicate a person or organization that is responsible for it, you will probably not find it to be reputable enough to be worth consulting. When this information is available, you will need to provide the name of the author or organization and the title of the site (probably abbreviated for your in-text references). Make certain that you provide in your list of works cited the entire electronic address (or URL). Because an electronic source is likely to change frequently, it's also crucial that you provide the date you consulted it.

When you take notes, make sure that you distinguish carefully between quoted words and your own words, and note the page number of print sources from which the information was taken. Copy all of the necessary information (as specified above) that would allow someone else to locate that source. Spare yourself the need to return to the library simply to find the name of the publisher or the page number from which a certain quotation or paraphrased information came. *One further caution*: it is not adequate merely to list a work you have used in your works cited. You must at all times make certain that it is clear what portion of your work has used what portion of the cited source.

Following sections of this book present ways to select and incorporate material into your work that are shared by all disciplines. Get into the habit now of employing the following suggestions. You will find that all of your writing will be stronger.

# WHEN DO YOU NEED TO ACKNOWLEDGE A SOURCE?

Some of what you write will come from your own observations and experience, some from class notes and discussion, some from what we call "common knowledge," some from the assigned readings in the course, some from works you've sought out on your own. Each of these sources merits a bit of discussion.

Obviously, you need not document in any formal way your own observations or experiences. The power of your own written voice should convince your readers of the plausibility of your own ideas and experiences.

## MATERIAL FROM CLASSROOM DISCUSSION

In most circumstances, you are free to incorporate ideas that have been explored in class discussion without worrying about the ownership of those ideas. Usually you may feel free to draw on background information presented in class as you provide a context for the more focused and developed discussion in your paper. If the class lecture or discussion itself has drawn on sources, such as films or readings, then you should attribute relevant ideas to their original source. But instructors do not expect or desire credit in your paper for ideas generated in class. Two suggestions:

1. Your own paper should probably not consist entirely of ideas repeated from class. Instead, it should develop ideas more fully or apply them in new ways that demonstrate your understanding of them. Ask your instructor for suggestions, if you are concerned that your paper may simply rehash ideas presented in class.

2. When you do rely on ideas or information from class, remember to explain them fully. Unless your professor specifies a particular kind of audience for your project, think of your reader as a person who is intelligent but who has not attended class. Anyone who picks up your paper should be able to understand it—not just the professor for whom you have written the paper.

## COMMON KNOWLEDGE

The category of information we call "common knowledge" is a more complex matter. Common knowledge includes broad historical facts that are not the conclusions or discoveries of a particular author, for example the fact that John Kennedy was the 35th President of the United States, or that Emily Brontë died the year after *Wuthering Heights* was published, or that under normal atmospheric pressure, water boils at 100 degrees Celsius. Even if you have to look up common-knowledge facts like these in a reference work, you do not need to cite your source. Nor do you have to document commonly known generalizations, such as the assumption that the Romantic Era in British literature was a time of intense literary innovation, or that computers have revolutionized communication, or that laboratory experimentation with animals is controversial. When you are beginning your studies of a particular subject, you might not always be able to tell easily what is common knowledge within a discipline and what isn't. But as you read more widely in a field with an eye toward what the other authors assume is shared information, you will be better able to assess what information properly belongs to particular authors. Two cautions:

1. Even if you judge a bit of information to be shared publicly, be careful not to represent another writer's phrasing of this common knowledge

as your own. Although the information may be common knowledge, a specific writer's expression of the information is still the property of that writer.

2. If you cannot decide if some information needs to be credited to an author, provide a reference giving such credit. When in doubt, cite your source.

Common knowledge also includes traditional tales, folk literature, and folk wisdom—tales or observations that are handed down without the knowledge of who wrote the tale or made the observation. Many fairy tales—for instance those of Mother Goose—or age-old songs and jokes—such as "Three Blind Mice" and "Why did the chicken cross the road?"—do not require documentation of the source. Nor would you need to provide a note crediting some source with the observation that a dog is a man's best friend, that absence makes the heart grow fonder, or that a bird in the hand is worth two in the bush. Many clichés or sayings fall into this category, though where authors are known, you should mention them. You should, for example, acknowledge that it was Alexander Pope who wrote "To err is human, to forgive divine," or Thomas Paine who wrote "These are the times that try men's souls." But generalized, commonsense observations do not usually need to be credited to a source. Be forewarned, however, that most readers will not continue reading something that tells them things they already know, and they will probably be irritated if your phrasing is hackneyed or your observations trite. If you use clichés in formal writing, use them in some fresh or unexpected way, or your readers will probably assume that you have nothing new to say and may lose interest in what you've written.

## USING TEXTBOOKS AS SOURCES

When you draw on information from a course textbook or from a source you have found on your own, you need to credit the source for all information drawn from it that is not common knowledge. For informal papers in which you refer only to class textbooks, professors may not demand that you give a complete reference that includes all of the publication facts. Ask your professor if it is acceptable merely to specify the author and title and put the page number from which the information was taken in parenthesis at the end of the sentence. Even if the source is a class textbook and the author and title are clear from the context (the assignment is a paper on *Wuthering Heights*, for example), you must at least cite the edition and page number because your professor will want to be able to locate the exact page from which you are getting the information, whether you quote it directly or paraphrase it. Even when you are writing a short "homework" or in-class assignment, you should acknowledge material that is not your own. You should provide proper citations of your sources not merely to avoid plagiarism, but to empower your writing with authority, evidence, and illustrative detail.

Remember to acknowledge the source of any visual material you've included in your essay, unless that material is truly in public domain or is provided by your word processing program as clip art. For example, if you incorporate photographs or drawings in your written project (and you did not create them), you must acknowledge the source of this material. A brief reference in a caption for the picture, followed by a full citation in your list of works cited, will usually suffice for class assignments.

## USING SOURCES IN CLASS PRESENTATIONS

In the give and take of ordinary class discussion, no one expects or desires attention to source material beyond mentioning an author's name or, at most, a page number of a book if others have copies of it with them. But a report to the class is a different matter. The more formal, lengthy, and public the presentation, the more thoroughly you should acknowledge the sources you've used.

If your report is entirely verbal (without use of PowerPoint or other visual material), acknowledge your use of information that is not common knowledge by referring to the name of the author of a publication as you present the information from that source. At the end of your talk, you can offer to share a printed list of the works you cite, a list that you should put in the proper format for the discipline. Such a practice doesn't add to the length of your talk, nor does it add any tedium or clutter. It demonstrates your care about ownership of ideas, and it adds to the authority of your comments by noting the studies you have consulted. Offering to share the citations list shows your respect not only for the published authors but for the other students in the course, as well.

If you are augmenting your presentation with PowerPoint, the visual text gives you a ready place to acknowledge source material. The PowerPoint text should not exactly duplicate what you are saying, or the effect will be redundant and tedious to your audience. You might signal the architecture of your talk with an outline, but you should resist the impulse to project your text as you speak it. In general, reserve the images you include for things that are best presented visually. You might want to display an important quotation that you're planning to discuss, and such a passage should include a citation of its source. You might use a diagram that illustrates relationships among the things you are discussing. If you use a diagram that you've found in print or on the Web, be certain to provide a full citation for it.

Whenever you include graphic materials, be very careful to assess the degree to which they are protected by copyright laws. Of course, you may use clip art as freely as you might any of the graphics enhancements that come with the software you're using. But if you include a photograph or a film or audio clip, you must acknowledge the proper source for the material. That source is probably not the search engine you employed to find it. For example, if you wanted an image of garment industry workers, you could conduct an image search on Google to find a wide assortment of images. If you choose one to use, the proper source to cite would not be Google—it would be the website that Google alerted you to. You should go to that site to find the name of the author or sponsoring organization, the title of the site, the URL and so forth. The same would be true for film clips or sound recordings that you are incorporating into your presentation. Make certain to find all of the information required for a full citation of the actual source, and include that citation (probably in a modestly sized font) on the screen during your presentation. Showing such care is important in establishing the authenticity of the materials you're including and in avoiding improper or unethical uses of published material. If you're using images, photos, and clips to complete a class project, make sure you acknowledge the proper source in proper form. In these circumstances, with this limited purpose and with proper citation, the law generally grants you this "fair use" of the material.

If your presentation is going to be posted on a course webpage or in any other way made available on the Internet, your use of such materials without proper citation could involve more than academic dishonesty. It could involve legal matters of violated copyright. Using such copyrighted material for purposes other than completion of an assignment for a class might require you to pay permissions fees and use specific language in your acknowledgments. Public and for-profit use of copyrighted tables, charts, poems, songs, film clips, sound recordings, and photographs nearly always requires written permission from the owner of the text.

# WHEN SHOULD YOU PARAPHRASE AND WHEN SHOULD YOU QUOTE?

Done properly, paraphrasing information gives you remarkable flexibility and, by permitting you to select only the information most relevant to your topic, it enables you to express your ideas with a minimum of verbiage. In short, it ensures that all of the information is pertinent, and it helps you to write with economy and vigor. When readers encounter information paraphrased or summarized from one of your sources, they do not have to move between writing by you and that by another author, shifting to a new voice, a new style, a different pace and context. When you paraphrase well, you do your reader a great service, because you've selected, organized, and phrased the information to suit your purposes, all in a manner that preserves a continuity of style and emphasis. But paraphrasing requires more work of you than simply copying someone else's words.

It is appropriate for you to paraphrase, instead of quoting, whenever the wording itself is less important to the purpose of your writing than the information it presents. If all you need from an economic study, for example, is the distressing information that, nationally, a woman with a college degree has the same earning potential as a male high school dropout, simply paraphrase the conclusions of the study in your own words and state your source, rather than quoting the study. Citing a statistic, a relatively unknown fact, a bit of information embedded in a study that otherwise is not relevant to your topic—in all of these situations, it is advisable to paraphrase rather than to quote.

Conversely, if the source itself is important to your topic, if the original wording helps you to illustrate your point, if the opinion expressed in the passage is controversial or highly unusual, or if the work itself *is* your subject (as in a paper on a literary work or an analysis of a text), then it is advisable to quote the actual words the original author used.

The next time you watch a televised news program, notice how the news writers use sources to establish the credibility of their reporting. The orchestrated movements to and from different locations, to and from other correspondents, other cameras and voices—these movements are analogous to an author's presentation of information in nonfiction writing. If they chose to, news anchors could present all of the news stories in their (or their news editor's) own words. Actually, doing so would provide better quality of both visual images and recorded language than the grainy, sometimes poorly focused film footage that is shot by foreign correspondents with their hand-held cameras in the heat of battle. Many news anchors do present much of the information themselves, particularly economic news (which doesn't film very dramatically) or stories for which they have no taped footage. But roughly half of the time, they turn the story over to a person in the field, to an eyewitness speaking without revising, or to a correspondent who narrates over some film footage, blurred by the processes of photography, distanced by the satellite transmission. Why? The answer is probably obvious. Going to the sources that are close to the story, to the people who are more authoritative than are the anchors themselves, contributes to their credibility. The news anchors become more authoritative for knowing when to let someone else be the authority. They introduce the news item and the taped footage, they let us know who is speaking, then they show us a tape, frequently following the segment with some kind of concluding remarks to give the story a sense of closure. Any edition of the evening news will demonstrate a similar use of primary source material. Even though the conventions of video documentation differ from those of printed writing—for example, there are no footnotes in a newscast—the purpose of such material is evident.

**Paraphrase** (with proper citations) when all you need is the information itself.

**Quote** when your source is important, when you can gain authority by turning to another author.

# HOW SHOULD YOU PARAPHRASE INFORMATION FROM A SOURCE?

Once you've decided that the occasion calls for paraphrasing, you need to do several things.

## SELECTING INFORMATION FROM YOUR SOURCE

First, you need to select the information relevant to your topic and make certain that you completely rephrase the ideas—in your own words. Do not use any phrases, syntax, or organization that appeared in the original work. These are the author's personal property, and representing segments or features of a passage as your own constitutes plagiarism.

### An Example of Paraphrasing

Suppose you are writing a paper on blue jeans as a cultural phenomenon, exploring what the enduring popularity of blue jeans illustrates about our culture. You find an essay in *American Heritage*, "The Jeaning of America—and the World," by Carin Quinn, in which she writes the following about Levi's jeans (on page 18):

> The pants have become a tradition, and along the way have acquired a history of their own—so much so that the company has opened a museum in San

Francisco. There was, for example, the turn-of-the-century trainman who re-placed a faulty coupling with a pair of jeans; the Wyoming man who used his jeans as a towrope to haul his car out of a ditch; the Californian who found sev-eral pairs in an abandoned mine, wore them, then discovered they were sixty-three years old and still as good as new and turned them over to the Smith-sonian as a tribute to their toughness. And then there is the particularly terrifying story of the careless construction worker who dangled fifty-two sto-ries above the street until rescued, his sole support the Levi's belt loop through which his rope was hooked.

You decide that the information about the museum and Quinn's examples of heroically strong jeans would strengthen your argument about what the jeans symbolize, and you write the following:

The jeans have earned a history all their own—to such an extent that the Levi's corporation even operates a museum of jeans in San Francisco. The museum presents the stories of the trainman who hitched two trains together with a pair of jeans, of the Wyoming man who towed his car out of ditch us-ing a pair of the jeans, of the Californian who found several pairs in an aban-doned mine, put them on, discovered they were still good as new after sixty-three years, and donated them to the Smithsonian as a tribute to their toughness. One especially horrifying story is that of the construction worker who lost his footing and dangled some fifty stories over the street, hanging only from the Levi's belt loop which his rope was hooked on. [improper para-phrase—plagiarism]

If you left this paragraph in your paper—even if you provided a note naming Carin Quinn as your source, and even if you didn't intend to deceive any-one—you would be guilty of plagiarism. Even though much of the paragraph has been rephrased, much of it hasn't been. This paragraph is organized ex-actly like the original, and much of the rewriting is merely substitution of syn-onyms for her original words, relying far too heavily on her syntax. The phrase "particularly terrifying," for example, is replaced by "especially horri-fying," with much of the original sentence left intact. The exact repetition of "found several pairs in an abandoned mine" and of the phrase "tribute to their toughness" is especially damning. If this wording is important enough to repeat verbatim, then you should quote it; otherwise, the passage should be completely reworded.

A far better example of paraphrasing, one that incorporates Quinn's ideas into the author's own argument, would be the following use of the material:

> Every morning, as you slip into your jeans, you put on a part of American history. You might merely be seeking warmth on a cold day or trying to make yourself decent for a walk downtown, but your jeans bring with them a long cultural tradition and probably more legendary strength than you'll ever need to run your errands. According to Carin Quinn, a pair of the original Levi's served once as a rope for a man in Wyoming who needed to tow his car from a ditch. A trainman once used a pair of the jeans to couple together two railway cars when the original coupling had broken. And when a hapless construction worker lost his footing fifty-two stories above the earth, one loop of his jeans was sufficient to hold him until help arrived (18). The Levi's corporation is well aware of its image. The leather patch with the Levi trademark shows a pair of jeans pulled between two horses. Most days you probably won't be repairing trains, dangling overhead, or deliberately frustrating the movement of horses, but wearing blue jeans symbolically connects you with the strength, ingenuity, preparedness, and even heroism embodied in these legends about the jeans.

Granted, this paragraph contains many ideas not found in the original source. And Quinn's paragraph presents information not included in this passage. But that's part of the point. You shouldn't simply repeat ideas you've found elsewhere; you should incorporate those ideas into a context all your own. And you should make clear which of the ideas in the paragraph derive from Quinn's work and which are entirely your own. Including the author's name at the beginning and a page or note number (depending on your style sheet) at the end of the paraphrased material makes it clear which information came from the source and which didn't. When you do find some useful information in a source you've consulted, you should explicitly name the author, select only those details that suit your purpose, phrase them in wording that is entirely your own, provide the page number, and then print the full publishing information in a list of works cited at the end of your paper.

## GIVING CREDIT TO YOUR SOURCE

The second thing you must do has already been mentioned but bears repeating here: Even if you are not quoting actual words, you need to give credit for the information, and you need to make clear exactly what has come from your source. Sometimes students believe that all they need to do if they've drawn information from a source is provide the author's name in parenthesis (or a note number) at the end of the paragraph containing the paraphrased material, confident that they've given credit where credit is due. This practice, however, is dangerously ambiguous and even misleading. A citation at the end of a paragraph implies that *all* of the material in the paragraph had its origin in the cited source, even if the paragraph is a mix of borrowed information and original insight. This practice might attribute ideas to the cited author that he or she did not develop, and it completely muddies the distinction between your own ideas and the author's. For example, in the last sample paragraph on jeans, if I had not mentioned the author's name where I did and if I had waited until the end of the paragraph to provide the page (or note) number, I would have inaccurately represented all of the ideas in the paragraph as Quinn's, thereby denying myself credit for the ideas that precede and follow the paraphrased material. Quinn does not make the observation that Levi's represents American ingenuity and preparedness for adversity. That idea is mine, and I shouldn't allow mere sloppiness with writing technique to rob me of credit for the discovery. The author's name at the beginning of the paraphrased material and the page number at the end of it function a bit as the beginning and ending quotation marks would if the material were quoted—they set off the cited information from your own, signaling its different status from the other words, identifying the source with maximum clarity and minimal distraction. In short, think of embedding the paraphrased material in your own prose as a kind of linguistic bracketing or fencing off of the information in as clear a way as possible, so as not to give the author too little credit—or too much.

## THE IMPORTANCE OF ACCURACY IN PARAPHRASING

Finally, you need to make certain that your synopsis of the author's ideas accurately reflects the author's actual statement. It probably goes without saying that you shouldn't misrepresent a paraphrased source, yet often students seem rather cavalier about restating others' ideas. Notice how frequently letters to the editor in your newspaper attempt to correct a perceived misreading or misrepresentation of an earlier letter. In the heat of the debate about social or political issues, people often say things imprecisely and misread the letters of others. Most of your sources are far more carefully composed than such letters. So should be your reading of them. Imagine that the authors whose words you are paraphrasing are going to read your synopsis of what they said. Will they feel that their views have been accurately and fairly represented? You may certainly disagree with what an author says in print, but it only helps to establish your credibility if you present those ideas fairly (maybe even quoting especially pertinent lines), before going on to demonstrate what is wrong with the author's position.

The focus and length of your project should guide you as you decide how much of the source you plan to use. It is usually best not to use only a general or concluding remark as if it is sufficient by itself to constitute evidence or argument. Neglecting to explain the author's reasons for her or his position and simply using a general phrase from the work will make it seem as if you are content to rely on authority assertions rather than to critically assess the ideas. Whether you agree with or challenge the published view (paraphrased or quoted), it helps you to establish your thoroughness and fairness if you attend to the reasoning behind an author's conclusions as you use the material.

# HOW SHOULD YOU QUOTE MATERIAL FROM A SOURCE?

## HOW MUCH TO QUOTE

Students sometimes wonder what proportion of their papers should be quoted material and what should be original words of their own. At one extreme, their papers might consist of lengthy quoted passages, stitched together with a few transitions of their own, as if writing is like assembling a patchwork quilt out of fragments of others' cloth. At the other extreme, students might quote only once, leaving most of their paragraphs without quotations to serve as illustration or evidence. Either extreme is disproportionate. Think of quoting as a valuable means of developing and supporting ideas—not as the means of presenting the ideas themselves. In some cases, quotations will be the best form your evidence could take, and neglecting to include relevant quotations could mean neglecting to provide convincing illustrative material. When you are revising your paper, read through it once without reading the quoted words. If your paper makes little sense without the quotations, you've probably attempted to make them do too much. Your words should present your argument; the quotations are only supportive material—valuable and essential to convincing your reader but never the primary means of presenting information.

## HOW TO PRESENT A QUOTATION

Once you've decided that it is appropriate to quote, you need to decide how much of the passage merits being presented in your paper. It may be that the information you need is entangled in a long sentence or paragraph, most of which is beside your immediate point. In this case, were you to quote the entire sentence or paragraph, you would needlessly divert your reader's attention from your immediate topic. You can quote passages of virtually any length: a word, a phrase, a sentence, even a paragraph. But whatever you quote should be entirely relevant to your purpose, and the longer the passage you quote, the greater should be your use of the material. Most of the time it would be rhetorically ineffective to quote a long passage, unless you plan to analyze or interpret it at some length, following the quotation. In most instances, your task will be to select a phrase or sentence that best illustrates the point you are making, and, taking great care to copy the material exactly as it is written, fit the quoted author's words into your own, making certain that you mark the quoted passage with quotation marks, name the source of the material (if it isn't already clear in the paragraph), and work the phrases into your own in a way that produces grammatical and coherent statements. If you fit a quoted phrase into a sentence, check for two things:

1. Between the opening and closing quotation marks, every symbol should be reproduced exactly at it appears in the original, unless you've clearly indicated what changes you made in the ways explained below.
2. Try reading your paragraph as if there were no quotation marks present. All of the words, quoted and unquoted, must function together in grammatical and coherent ways.

Never present a quotation as a completely separate sentence. Always introduce it in some way. The presence of quotation marks (without any introduction or transition) is not a sufficient signal that the material has come from a source, because writers use quotation marks for some purposes other than quoting. They might mark a word that they are using in a special way or mark a word that they are discussing. When I mentioned "common knowledge" above, I put it in quotation marks, because I was discussing what the phrase means. Some authors who need to use a slang expression will surround the expression with quotation marks as if to apologize for using the phrase. It is not a particularly admirable practice, but it is a fairly common one. Don't "fly off the handle" at such practices; instead, keep your "cool." The important point here is to introduce all quotations in ways that indicate you are quoting, that identify the source, and that suggest the significance of what the person is saying.

As you lead into a quoted passage, you should consider what sorts of information about your source the reader needs to know to understand the significance of the quotation.

- Does the author have a position or credentials that are relevant to the quoted statement?
- Is the date of the statement important enough to note as you introduce it?
- Was the quoted passage published originally as a part of a major study?
- Has the author employed a particular research methodology that might contextualize the study within the field?
- Has the author made use of important or unusual materials?
- Is the journal or other medium in which the piece appears particularly noteworthy?

If you know this kind of information and it helps to establish the context of the material within the field of your topic, you should consider including it as you introduce a quoted passage. Think of the reasons that you consulted the source in the first place and the reasons why you selected the passage that you did.

If you can signal these reasons to your reader as you introduce the material, your reader might better understand the relationship of the quoted passage to your essay. At the very least, you should convey that the quoted material comes from a source:

"According to one study ... "
"One author puts it this way ... "
"A later report claims that ... "

Better yet, name the source:

"Miller argues that . . . "
"Johnston, who studied the mosquito for fifteen years, postulates that . . . "
"The chief engineer on the project, Eliza Swaney, observes . . . "

And if the passage is important, alert your reader to the nature of its significance or to its context in your work:

"Jonathan Alder offers a contrasting view . . . "
"Linkholder's rebuttal shows her dependence on Connelly's theorem . . . "
"Note the veiled anger in Cramer's reply . . . "

Your objective is to signal your movements to and from a quotation with maximum clarity, continuity, and context, and to encourage your reader to predict what will follow in a quotation. As you read authors you admire in the field for which you are writing, get in the habit of noticing how the authors have chosen to do what they do. When you encounter writing done well, read it carefully, not just for the information you need, but to learn from the example alternate ways of meeting your needs as a writer.

## HOW TO SHOW ADDITIONS
## AND DELETIONS IN A QUOTATION

Between the opening set of quotation marks and the closing pair, every word, letter, and punctuation mark must be exactly as it appears in the original. You can change some of the things in a quotation—adding or deleting words—but only if you indicate that you have done so and only if your change does not distort the meaning of what you've quoted. One change is permitted—actually required—within a quotation: If the source itself quotes something else, you change the double quotation marks to single ones, so that they are not confused with the ones that you have provided. You may also change the final punctuation mark in your quotation of a passage to suit your own grammatical needs (see below), in effect stopping your quoting before the final symbol. But if grammar demands that you add a word, change the tense of a quoted verb, or clarify the reference of a quoted pronoun, for instance, you should do so by enclosing your change in square brackets (not parentheses). If you are using a typewriter and it does not have square brackets, [ or ], leave spaces as you type where the brackets should be and write them in neatly in black ink.

If for reasons of clarity, grammar, or brevity, you decide to delete a word or phrase from within a series of quoted words, put in its place an ellipsis, three spaced dots . . . , to show your reader that you've left something out. If you are quoting a passage that itself already makes use of an ellipsis, place the periods you add within square brackets to distinguish between those you added to show your deletion and those already in the text you quote. In this situation, you should space once before the opening bracket, *between* the periods themselves, and once after the closing bracket, so that your ellipsis looks like this: [. . .] If the passage you are quoting does not already make use of an ellipsis, simply add the required periods without the brackets. If quoting the passage requires extensive bracketing and ellipses, to the extent that you must undergo all sorts of grammatical or typographic contortions, consider paraphrasing the material or quoting only the most relevant phrases or words. The following examples will illustrate how to use square brackets and the ellipsis.

Assume for the moment that you are writing an essay on Fitzgerald's *The Great Gatsby*, exploring the ways in which the narrator, Nick Carraway, is biased as he relates the events. Because your topic is a work of literature, and especially because you are attempting to show how the narrator's language reveals his attitudes, you will frequently wish to quote from the novel. You will find no more direct source of evidence to convince skeptical readers than quoting the actual novel.

## Using Square Brackets to Mark Words Added to a Quotation

**Original** (from page 39 of Fitzgerald's *The Great Gatsby*):
In his blue gardens men and girls came and went like moths among the whisperings and the champagne and the stars.

**Your use of the passage** (the page number follows the passage):
Nick Carraway, the narrator in the novel, says that "In his [Gatsby's] blue

~~gardens men and girls came and went like moths among the whisperings~~
and the champagne and the stars" (39).

*Explanation*

By itself, the original "his" in the passage would have incorrectly implied that
the gardens under discussion were Nick's instead of Gatsby's. In this case, a
more graceful way of clarifying the meaning of the pronoun would be to provide a referent for "his" as you introduce the quotation, as in the following:

> Early in the novel, Nick reveals his contempt for Gatsby's guests: "In his
> blue gardens men and girls came and went like moths among the whis-
> perings and the champagne and the stars" (39).

This use of the material avoids the clutter of the brackets and better alerts the
reader to notice Nick's judgment of the guests. Yet another way to use this material (and other relevant details from the novel) might be to write the following:

> Despite Nick's early claim that he is "inclined to reserve all judgments"
> (1), he says that Tom has "a cruel body" (7), and he refers to Gatsby's
> guests as "moths" (39).

This might be an even better use of the material, depending on the focus
and context of the essay. It explains why it matters that Nick is in fact judg-
mental, and it makes use of selected phrases or words that illustrate this trait.
Within the pairs of quotation marks, every word is identical to the original.
And each quotation is followed by the number of the page on which the passage appears. If you can rework your use of a passage to avoid using the
brackets, do so. But if you need to change something, employ the brackets to
signify that change. Following is one more example of how bracketed information may clarify the meaning of a pronoun. While it is clear in the novel
that Nick is speaking of Gatsby in these lines, removing the passage from its
context requires that you clarify the meaning in your context.

**Original** (from page 102):
For several weeks I didn't see him or hear his voice on the phone—mostly
I was in New York, trotting around with Jordan and trying to ingratiate

myself with her senile aunt—but finally I went over to his house one Sunday afternoon.

**Your use of the material:**
Nick makes it clear that the only events of that summer that interest him now are those involving Gatsby. At one point he alludes to other events, but he quickly returns to his real subject:

> For several weeks I didn't see him [Gatsby] or hear his voice on the phone—mostly I was in New York, trotting around with Jordan and trying to ingratiate myself with her senile aunt—but finally I went over to his house one Sunday afternoon. (102)

Here Nick summarizes "several weeks" in only nineteen words, those weeks not mattering because they didn't involve his hero, Gatsby.

*Explanation*

Notice again the simple way you can clear up a potentially confusing pronoun with information enclosed in brackets. Notice also that, when the quoted passage is relatively long (more than three typed lines), you present it in "block" format: you set it off from the rest of your text by indenting it. When you present block quotations, you should not enclose the material in quotation marks unless they appear in the original. Setting it off in block format already tells the reader that the material is quoted. The page number or any other parenthetical publication information follows the period in a block quotation. Notice also that the paragraph does not end simply because I presented a block quotation. I followed the passage with attention to its details, connecting it to the idea I'm developing. Beginning and closing lines in paragraphs are positions of extreme emphasis; don't leave your reader dangling at the end of block quotations. Resume your analysis, closing the paragraph by returning to your immediate point.

If your paper is written in the present tense and you wish to quote something written in the past tense, bracket the part of the verb you change:

**Original** (from page 80):
He had waited five years and bought a mansion where he dispensed starlight to casual moths—so that he could "come over" some afternoon to a stranger's garden.

---

Your use of the material:
Nick implies throughout the novel that Gatsby's guests are undeserving of his social efforts, saying that Gatsby "dispense[s] starlight to casual moths" (80).

Notice, as always, the quoted material is introduced in some way that makes its source and its importance clear to your reader.

## Using the Ellipsis to Indicate That You Deleted Words from a Quotation

If you decide, in the interests of brevity and relevance, to leave out some material from within a quoted passage, provide the ellipsis (three spaced periods) to show it. The deletion, obviously, should not change the meaning of the passage, nor should it produce a series of words that do not fit grammatically with the rest of your writing. If you are omitting an entire sentence or more from within a quotation, you should provide the regular period at the end of the sentence before the deleted material, and then provide the usual ellipsis (three spaced periods) to show that one or more sentences have been deleted. Do not begin or end a quotation with ellipses, especially if you are quoting only a word or a phrase. Surrounding the quoted material with ellipses only adds unnecessary clutter. If the passage itself already contains an ellipsis, place the ellipsis within square brackets. The brackets will enable your reader to distinguish between the ellipsis you have added and the spaced periods used for some other purpose by the author of the original passage.

Suppose you are writing an essay on the psychology behind the marketing of sport utility vehicles. You find an essay by Malcolm Gladwell called "Big and Bad: How the S.U.V. Ran Over Automotive Safety" (*The New Yorker*, 12 January 2004). Because Gladwell incorporates in his essay various studies and interviews with automotive marketing specialists, you decide to use some of the material from following passage:

**Original** (from page 31):
The S.U.V. boom represents, then, a shift in how we conceive of safety—from active to passive. It's what happens when a larger number of drivers

conclude, consciously or otherwise, that the extra thirty feet that the Trail-Blazer takes to come to a stop doesn't really matter, that the tractor-trailer will hit them anyway, and that they are better off treating accidents as inevitable rather than avoidable. "The metric that people use is size," says Stephen Popiel, a vice-president of Millward Brown Goldfarb, in Toronto, one of the leading automotive market-research firms. "The bigger something is, the safer it is. In the consumer's mind, the basic equation is, If I were to take this vehicle and drive it into this brick wall, the more metal there is in front of me the better off I'll be."

**Your use of the material:**

One of the reasons that S.U.V.s are so profitable to manufacture is that, classified as trucks, they need not meet government safety standards established for passenger cars. Yet nearly all of the advertisements for S.U.V.s promote safety as the vehicles' chief advantage. Seated far from the road, surrounded by massive expanses of cushioned plastic and many of the amenities of home, drivers of S.U.V.s certainly *feel* safe, despite the loss of maneuverability and braking power as the size and weight of vehicles increase. "The S.U.V. boom," according to Malcolm Gladwell, "represents . . . a shift in how [American drivers] conceive of safety—from active to passive." A passive view of safety reflects a general assumption that people don't have much control over what happens to them, so they should be prepared for the worst and treat "accidents as inevitable rather than avoidable." Gladwell quotes market-researcher Stephen Popiel: "The metric that people use is size. . . . The bigger something is, the safer it is" (31). As people feel safer and less responsible for what happens, they do things they'd do if they *weren't* driving—talking on the phone, watching videos, reaching for the nearby cup-holder. As Gladwell notes, "That feeling of safety isn't the solution; it's the problem" (32).

*Explanation*

This passage illustrates a number of things. In the first quoted line, an ellipsis replaces the word "then," a transition in Gladwell's essay that doesn't function well in the new context. The deleted word is within a single quoted sentence, so there's no added period—only the three required for an ellipsis.

This ellipsis is not placed in square brackets because Gladwell's original passage contains no ellipsis of his own. Replacing Gladwell's "we" with the bracketed "American drivers" keeps the point of view consistent with the third person used in the rest of the paragraph. The brackets acknowledge the change. Because the same page of Gladwell's essay is used again twice in the same paragraph, the page number is not presented until the final use of the material. It will be clear that the quotations are from the same page. Note that the page number is not part of the quotation but it is part of the sentence, so it is placed after the quotation marks but before the period. In general, select what is relevant and important enough to quote; use the ellipsis to indicate that you have left out material within the original; place the ellipsis within square brackets only if the original passage itself uses spaced periods; use square brackets to designate material added to the original; introduce quoted sources explicitly in your text; make certain that all words (quoted and un-quoted) fit together in grammatically complete ways; and provide page numbers (of print sources) after the quotation marks but before the final punctuation of the sentence.

With the proper symbols, you can add, replace, or delete words within quoted material and enjoy considerable flexibility in the way you use quotations. In general, try to keep your use of quotations as straightforward and uncomplicated as you can. Your reader should always be able to tell what has been taken verbatim from a source and what you have done to change the material. Next are a few more suggestions for punctuating quotations within your work.

# HOW SHOULD YOU PUNCTUATE QUOTATIONS?

## INTRODUCING A QUOTATION

If you are introducing a quotation with a grammatically complete statement (an independent clause), follow the opening with a colon:

> According to Naomi Klein, the increase in the power of corporations can be traced back to a single, seemingly harmless idea that was popular in the mid-1980s: "that successful corporations must primarily produce brands, as opposed to products" (3).

In this example, the part of the sentence that precedes the colon is grammatically complete. It could end where the colon is without resulting in a sentence fragment. A colon is the proper punctuation mark only if what precedes the colon is grammatically complete. What follows the colon may be a word, a phrase, a sentence, or even a paragraph.

Use a comma if what you are quoting is a complete sentence but your introduction to it makes the quotation itself the necessary object of a verb:

> He said, "I never met her before that occasion."

In this sentence, the verb "said" requires an object (in this case the quotation itself). "He said" is grammatically incomplete, so it is followed by a comma, not a colon. Rephrased as a complete sentence, the introductory phrase requires a colon:

His denial was emphatic: "I never met her before that occasion."

In the above sentence, if a comma followed the word "emphatic," the result would be a comma splice, because two grammatically independent clauses would be joined without a conjunction.

When you quote single words or phrases from an author, your punctuation should be exactly the same as if the quotation marks were not there. Don't insert unnecessary commas. As I did above, when I wrote that Nick called Gatsby's guests "moths," you should simply use the quoted word without any preceding comma.


## ENDING A QUOTATION

At the end of a quoted passage, you should provide whatever end punctuation serves your grammatical needs. If you stop quoting from a passage that ends with a punctuation mark, you may drop the original punctuation mark and provide whatever is grammatically appropriate within your text. In American usage, commas and periods are always placed *inside* the final set of quotation marks, unless you provide a page number in parenthesis after the quotation. Note the difference in the two following examples:

Throughout *America's Meltdown*, John Arden calls American culture the lowest common denominator or "LCD society."

John Arden calls American culture the lowest common denominator or "LCD society" (1).

The page number in parentheses is not part of the quotation, so it is placed outside the quotation marks, but it is part of the sentence, so it precedes the final period. Semicolons, colons, question marks, and exclamation points always appear *outside* the final quotation marks (unless the question mark or exclamation is part of the quotation).

## PRESENTING QUOTATIONS WITHIN QUOTATIONS

When you quote a passage that itself uses quotation marks, change the author's original double quotation marks to single ones to indicate a quotation within a quotation:

**Original** (from page 7 of Rachel Carson's *The Silent Spring*):
Since the mid-1940s over 200 basic chemicals have been created for use in killing insects, weeds, rodents, and other organisms described in the modern vernacular as "pests"; and they are sold under several thousand different brand names.

**Your use of the material:**
According to Rachel Carson, more than 200 chemicals are used to kill "organisms described in the modern vernacular as 'pests'" (7).

Notice that the original double quotation marks are changed to single ones to distinguish them from the ones you've provided. Because the quoted passage is presented in the text, instead of set off in block format, the page number is placed outside the quotation marks but before the period. If no page number were provided, the final period would be placed inside *both* sets of closing quotation marks.

## PUNCTUATING TITLES

Whenever you provide the title of a work, you should punctuate it properly. Titles of long works, originally published independently, should be underlined (or italicized). Titles of novels, magazines, plays, books, television shows, films, and speeches are all underlined. Titles of essays, short poems, short songs, articles, episodes from a television series, and short stories are all placed in quotation marks. If you quote a published review that punctuates titles differently, you may change the way the title is presented in what you quote without indicating that you have done so. Most magazines, for example, put titles of films in quotation marks. If you quote such a review, you should underline the title or italicize it to attain stylistic consistency in what you've written.

## QUOTING POETRY

One final situation needs explanation here: quoting lines of poetry. One important difference between poetry and prose is that lines of poetry are usually shorter than the full printed width of the paper. The line breaks are an important feature of the poem's form. Thus, if you are quoting a section of a poem that, in the original, runs onto another line, you should indicate where the line ends by providing a spaced slash mark where the break occurs. For example, the opening sentence in Adrienne Rich's "Diving into the Wreck" reads (lines 1–7),

> First having read the book of myths,
> and loaded the camera,
> and checked the edge of the knife-blade,
> I put on
> the body-armor of black rubber
> the absurd flippers
> the grave and awkward mask.

If you wish to quote the entire sentence, present it in block format, as I did above, preserving all of the original spacing and line breaks (without slash marks). If you wish to quote fewer than three lines, present them as part of your regular paragraph (not in block format), but provide slash marks to show where her original lines were broken, as in the following example:

> In her poem "Diving into the Wreck," Adrienne Rich assumes that our history of the past is a largely fictionalized "book of myths," a metaphoric place that is dangerous for the female explorer because historians have traditionally neglected the actions of women in their accounts of our past. To document what really occurred in history, she "loaded the camera" to record the events, she "checked the edge of the knife-blade" that she might need to protect herself or to pry beneath superficial appearances, and she put on "the body-armor of black rubber / the absurd flippers / the grave and awkward mask." To Rich, exploring the past is a dangerous but valuable enterprise that requires much preparation.

This paragraph illustrates much of the same selection and introduction of the quoted material that I discussed earlier. The relevant phrases have all been grammatically worked into the author's own phrasing, so that all the words, quoted and original, produce grammatical and coherent sentences. When the quoted lines break in the original, those breaks have been marked with spaced slash marks. Marking such breaks in this fashion is important only in quoting lines of poetry within your regular text, and failure to do so ignores an important feature of the original poem.

## QUOTATION MARKS AND OTHER PUNCTUATION

Below are some more examples that illustrate a variety of punctuation circumstances.

**A semicolon following a quotation:**
Nick calls Gatsby's guests "moths"; perhaps he is not so impartial after all.

**A colon following a quotation:**
Emma cited several reasons for what she called her "unrestrained rage": Cathy's arrogance, Tom's indifference, and Jackie's boredom.

**A quotation with an exclamation point and parenthetical page number:**
The technician said, "That lapse in procedure is inexcusable!" (16).

**A quotation with an exclamation point followed by attribution:**
"That lapse in procedure is inexcusable!" said the technician (16).

**A quoted question:**
The task force sought to answer one question: "Why did the bridge collapse?"

**A quoted question and parenthetical page number:**
In *The Culture of Fear*, Barry Glassner asks, "Why, as crime rates plunged throughout the 1990s, did two-thirds of Americans believe they were soaring?" (xi).

**A quoted phrase that is part of a question you ask:**

At what point did the corporation become entirely self-serving and no longer a "public institution whose purpose was to serve national interests and advance the public good" (Bakan 153)?

# HOW SHOULD YOU SELECT AND CITE ELECTRONIC AND INTERNET SOURCES?

The Internet and the proliferation of other electronic and online resources have made information more readily available than ever before. But the variety of such materials has also greatly increased the need for you to critically assess the information you find. The ease with which you can move from site to site, click on links, shrink and open new windows, and cut and paste information to notepads or to documents—this rapid movement from source to source practically *encourages* sloppy and unethical uses of copyrighted information and wording. The format of the Web creates the dangerous illusion that the items you find on it are free and/or public property, akin to common knowledge that isn't owned by an author. Unlike printed material in a library, the information on an electronic source is subject to frequent change, and if you haven't been careful to copy all of the information you will need at the time you see it (or better yet, printed a hard copy of the page), you might lose your access to it, if the text has been revised. A Web page might not even list an author's name, and a particular page to which you might have been linked might not present any publishing information or context for the material on your screen.

Browsing the Web seems like—and often *is*—a form of leisurely entertainment, and your habits during recreation can have dire consequences if they spill over into your writing and suspend the careful sorts of critical thinking and responsible note-taking that are essential to responsible professional and academic writing. Further, the visual similarities among different kinds of documents, when all are filtered through a browser or computer, tend to blur distinctions among them, to make them all seem equal in their reliability or authority. But there are extreme differences among the kinds of material you can view online. Despite all of these challenges, you can learn to sort the nonsense and idiocy from the truly relevant and reputable, and you can use the information with the same scrutiny and care that persuasive writers learn to apply to all that they read.

Much of the early praise for the potential of the Internet focused on the freedom of access to it as a means of publishing—as if the Internet represented the full realization of a democracy in which all people could publish and read virtually everything. At a local level, that freedom takes the form of policies of many Internet service providers that grant all subscribers some space on the server to launch their own websites. In effect, anyone who subscribes to an Internet service may post information.

One practical effect of this accessibility is that the millions of documents and images available from a terminal represent a complete mix of wholly valuable and reputable information with information that is biased, deceptive, or totally unimportant. With careful attention to the source, meticulous critical assessment of evidence and authority, and some detective work, you may find highly useful and credible information related to your topic. For example, major newspapers, magazines, and news organizations usually have websites—often electronic editions of or supplements to their publications and broadcasts. When you know the agency or organization that hosts the site, and the site has been assembled with the same care and editorial standards as the organization's other work, you may rely on the website with as much confidence as you would the print publication or broadcast.

Intermixed with online journals are countless commercial sites, individuals' Web pages and blogs, university sites, government sites, nonprofit agency pages, and highly varied other electronic forums for exchange of information. A United States government electronic archive of Senate hearings might be a click or two away from a child's hobby page. Readings posted on the Web by a professor might seem to blend seamlessly with essays written by her students. Always consider the source. The nature of your topic will assist you in determining if a particular site is relevant to your project.

## SOURCE RELIABILITY: A SAMPLE TOPIC

An example will illustrate a few of the challenges involved in assessing the reliability of websites. Suppose you are writing an essay on the proposal to permit exploratory drilling for oil in Alaska's Arctic National Wildlife Refuge (ANWR). Entering "ANWR oil exploration" in any of the large Internet search engines (*Yahoo*, for example) will yield links to many related sites. The sheer variety of them should suggest that you need to choose a highly precise focus to make the topic manageable in an essay. That proposal involves issues of natural resource preservation, the international oil market, national security, electoral politics, ecological effects (themselves a highly varied lot), effects on other regional industries (like salmon), anthropological concerns, and a host of other issues. If your topic is any one of these, you will need to sift through contentious and contradictory claims by the involved parties: the oil corporations, the political figures (national and state), interest groups (on many sides), scientists, economists, lawyers, indigenous peoples, labor unions, and environmentalists. Many of these sources will simply be too biased by self-interest to serve as reputable authorities. But if your essay focuses on the conduct of the arguments themselves, on the *rhetoric* of some focused aspect of the debate, then virtually any of these sources could become primary material. The language and argument employed by various parties could become your topic as they illustrate various techniques of argument and propaganda.

A fifteen-minute search of the topic reveals that the national interest in this proposal has energized public relations efforts on the part of industry and environmental groups—to name just two general sides in the debate. The sophistication of such efforts complicates one's attempts to find balanced discussions of the topic—at least on Internet sites. The well-funded participants in this debate have learned the advantages of paying for prominence in the search engine results. Many of the links that appear among the first ten on Google or Yahoo have not been selected by an impartial search program according to their relevance. Google and Yahoo are commercial sites that sell those positions. You will need to search with varied keywords and scroll through many pages of results to find different perspectives. There is certainly no correlation between a site's placement in the search results and its reliability as an authority for research purposes.

You should pay attention to the URL domain of the sites you find—the kind of abbreviation that follows the dot, whether "com," "net," "org," "edu," or "gov." The advocacy groups—whether for the oil industry or for environmental concerns—realize that readers are rightly suspicious of sites with a ".com" domain, as this signifies the for-profit purpose of the site. So they've formed organizations or connections with universities that permit them to use ".org" and ".edu" domains. On a politically charged topic like oil exploration in Alaska, it might also be the case that United States government sites (with "gov" domains) are urging particular policies or legislative initiatives. The management of public information is, of course, a strategic effort—one that may or may not yield reliable information with a basis in fact. Little is as it appears to be in the cyberspace battle for public opinion. Remaining skeptical, seeking evidence of bias or agenda, and being persistent in identifying the members and missions of organizations will be crucial whenever you're looking at Web resources on complicated, hot national topics.

Most of the websites discussing Alaskan oil exploration foreground their credibility in sometimes transparent ways. For example, one site, called simply "anwr.org," describes its parent organization, Arctic Power, as a "grassroots, non-profit citizen's organization with 10,000 members founded in April of 1992 . . ." ("Arctic Power"). The organization emphasizes how comprehensive its membership is:

> Arctic Power membership spans the economic spectrum—including miners, fishermen, loggers, tourism operators, transportation businesses, labor unions, banks, teachers, the legal community, retail firms, service industries, non-profit organizations, Alaska Native corporations, local elected officials, and many others. ("Arctic Power")

The prominent links on its home page certainly make it seem as if it's got this complicated issue covered, attending to veterans, labor, Alaskans, and even caribou. But all of these topics are discussed with one mission in mind: "to expedite congressional and presidential approval of oil exploration and production within the Coastal Plain of the Arctic National Wildlife Refuge" ("Arctic Power"). The board of directors for Arctic Power includes representatives of the Alaska Support Industry Alliance, the Alaska State Chamber of Commerce, the Resource Development Council, the Alaska Miner's Association, and the Alaska Oil & Gas Association. On the one hand, having such members on its board gives the group insight into corporate positions on the issue. On the other, it casts doubt on the extent to which the group is truly a "grassroots" movement, representing a citizen's initiative. Its site offers brief arguments, sometimes called "talking points," in quick tours of the topic. And it asks readers to use its "Action Center" to e-mail Congressional representatives, to petition Congress, and to blog in support of oil drilling. The rhetoric of the site is a mix of seeming neutrality and energetically partisan advocacy. Like other oil-industry funded groups with "org" domains, this one works to gain credibility as a moderate group with broad support, and then engages in passionate and one-sided argument.

Similar strategies are employed by groups opposing Alaska drilling, as well. One such group, The Alaska Coalition, describes itself as a "coalition of nearly 1000 conservation, sporting, labor, and religious groups working together to protect Alaska's wild public land" ("Who We Are"). Claiming to be born of cooperation among nearly a thousand organizations with highly varied missions, the Alaska Coalition offers an organizational self-portrait drawn with many of same strokes as those used by Arctic Power: cooperation, diversity, populism. And like the site of Arctic Power, the Alaska Coalition's site offers talking points, links to other activist groups, and calls for action and public support—but for conservation not drilling. There are sites more oriented toward information than bandwagon activism, such as one maintained by Ecotrust calling itself "Inforain," a "bioregional information system" ("About Inforain"). Though this site is better documented, calmer, and far more substantive than the Alaska Coalition's site, it is very much a proconservation site and therefore a partisan in the debate.

When you choose a topic fraught with controversy, you need to seek varied points of view and pay meticulous attention to the sorts of evidence provided by the sources and the overall validity of the reasoning they employ. Check the credentials of the principal authors, and attempt to verify the information they provide by consulting additional sources, ideally universities, major news organizations, print publications (ones without economic ties to the interested parties), government documents, and court reports. As this sample topic illustrates, you should be cautious and skeptical of all claims— doubly so when the source is online. The Web has evolved into an enterprise that is chiefly commercial. You should not limit your research to Internet sites, unless such texts are well suited to your topic.

## CITING INTERNET WEBSITES

Citing paraphrased or quoted information from Internet sources requires some adaptation of your usual procedures. If you know the name of the author or of the organization, name it in your text as you introduce the material, mentioning the publication medium as you do so (website, CD-ROM, online journal, and so forth). If you are using a particular page from a website, place the title of the page in quotation marks in parentheses at the end of the sentence. Titles of pages or sections within sites are often quite long, and quoting them in your text in their entirety would be cumbersome. In such cases, you need to preserve the first word of the section name (to enable your readers to easily identify it among your list of works cited) and then use an abbreviated or shortened form that refers to the full citation in your list. Writing an abbreviated title isn't always a simple matter. For example, an underlined link on the Natural Resources Defense Council "Wilderness Preservation" page is entitled "In Big Oil's Crosshairs." The page itself, if you click on that link, is headed "The Bush Administration's Unbalanced Plan to Drill in the Western Arctic." In this case, the best thing might be simply to use "Bush Administration's Unbalanced Plan," making certain that the actual full citation is clear in your list of works cited. The format for listing Web pages and sites will differ according to the appropriate style manual for your discipline. And, because the kinds of sources continue to evolve, most of the style manuals offer only provisional guidance and admit that the guidelines will be changing as the media evolve. But all the formats require that your final list include the author or organization (if known), the title of the page, the complete URL (Universal Resource Locator), the latest date that the page was updated (if known), and the date you actually consulted it.

The convenience of consulting websites has two costs: the need to be particularly alert to various ways the sites might be unreliable, and the challenges of citing sometimes tricky documents. It's not always easy to tell who the author is, and you might not find a date that the document was last revised—though you should explore other links on the home page to try to find this information. You may not know whether a title should be presented as a part of a whole (and placed in quotation marks) or as a site on its own (and underlined or italicized). Remember to consult the latest edition of the style manual for the discipline in which you are writing, and make certain that you do two things:

1. Provide the complete URL, with totally accurate transcription of every symbol (including slash marks and underlines) as it appears in the location box of your browser. If it is so long that you must break the line, do so only *after* one of the slash marks. The Modern Language Association asks that you enclose the URL in angle brackets, < >, to clearly signify its status.
2. Make certain that you provide the date that you consulted the site. Below are citations as they would appear in a list of works cited in MLA format:

**A reference to a website:**

Arctic Monitoring and Assessment Programme (AMAP) Homepage. 2 August 2006. AMAP. 2 August 2006. <http://www.amap.no>.

**A reference to one page from a website:**

"Asthma and Air Pollution." 8 June 2005. Natural Resources Defense Council. 2 August 2006. <http://www.nrdc.org/health/effects/fasthma.asp>.

## OTHER ELECTRONIC SOURCES

Your computer might be linked to some databases to which your university or employer subscribes. Because you gain access to these databases with your Internet browser, they might seem like ordinary websites, but they are actually distinct from the Internet. One such database is *LexisNexis Academic*, frequently available on campuses. LexisNexis offers searchable, computerized archives of published documents. This powerful—and expensive—service is a highly useful means of gaining access to electronic versions of materials originally published in a variety of media: newspapers, magazines, journals, newsletters, trade publications, and abstracts. LexisNexis enables you to view and print information directly from your computer without the need to find the printed source in a library. It provides the actual written texts from the original sources but without the graphics, visual layout, and pagination of the originals. Generally believed to be reputably edited and reliable texts, the items found on *LexisNexis Academic* are really distinct versions of the original works. The service does provide the full publication information for the items, but it reformats the document in ways that do not enable you to tell on which page in the document a given sentence or paragraph appears. Because the item has been significantly reformatted from its original form, you must cite the version you consulted, indicating that the material was obtained through LexisNexis. Presumably, the actual words have been transcribed accurately by the editors, but the authority for the accuracy of that transcription now resides at LexisNexis. Your citation should indicate that the online service owns the version you consulted and that what you cite is at one stage of remove from the original printed text.

When consulting such an archive, you need to make yourself familiar with how it works—both with how the search engine enables you to make choices among dates and kinds of materials and with how the service organizes and labels the parts of the original citation. The author's name might be called the "byline"; the title of an article might be called the "headline." The services offer guidance and tips that enable you to figure out how the original citation would be reconstructed from what they provide, and most include a link to some sample citations following various formats. When you cite in your regular text a source obtained through one of these services, use the author's name (if available) or the title, as you would if you were citing the original version. This reference, whether explicit or parenthetical, should clearly identify to which item in your list of works cited the name refers. Unless the service provides the original page numbers, you do not provide them. In your list of works cited, begin by citing the work as you would the original, and then follow it by noting the name of the online service, the name of the institution that subscribed to that service and its location, the date you found the source on the site, and the URL for the site in angle brackets. Consult the appropriate style sheet for your discipline for the exact way of listing such a source. If you've found an item on a service such as *LexisNexis Academic* and have not consulted the original version, you must not cite it without acknowledging the online source.

Other subscription databases that are frequently available at libraries include *InfoTrac* (by Thomson Learning), *Academic Search Premier* and *Business Source Complete* (by EBSCOhost), and *ProQuest*. Like *LexisNexis*, they present the full texts of documents but reformat them in ways that do not preserve the original layout and pagination. Because the original page number for a passage will not be identified by these databases, parenthetical citations to such sources usually will consist of only the author's name. The entry in the list of works cited must acknowledge that the version of the document you consulted was provided by the database. The URL for the actual document is probably long and complicated, often a series of symbols and letters that is a temporary designation. For this reason, you provide the URL for the database, not the one for the document itself.

If the database provides scanned images of the original pages of the publication, as is sometimes done with articles from scholarly journals, then you should provide the page number in your parenthetical citation as you normally would. In your works cited, you still must cite the online archive or service that provided the scanned image. *JSTOR* (Journal Storage) is one such archive. Operated by a nonprofit organization, the *JSTOR* collection spans nearly every discipline and is continually expanding. It does not include current issues of scholarly publications. There is likely to be a gap of several years between the most recent issue and those included in the archive. The *JSTOR* archive greatly expands the availability of scholarly journals and the ease with which they may be consulted. It is crucial that you acknowledge the archive as you cite sources obtained with it—not only to be academically honest but also to support the service.

Below are some citations of documents from subscription databases in MLA format.

Barash, Jeffrey Andrew. "The Sources of Memory." *Journal of the History of Ideas* 58 (1997): 707–17. *JSTOR*. 2 August 2006 <http://www.jstor.org/search>.
"Consumers Consider the Importance of Corporate Social Responsibility." *Strategic Finance* August 2006: 20–22. *Business Source Complete*. EBSCOhost. Denison University, Granville, OH. 6 August 2006 <http://search.ebscohost.com>.
Dunn, Joseph. "How Electric Cars Came Back from the Dead." *Sunday Times (London)* 23 July 2006: 6. *LexisNexis Academic*. LexisNexis. Denison University, Granville, OH. 6 August 2006 <http://web.lexis-nexis.com/universe>.
Livingstone, Sonia and Ellen J. Helsper. "Does Advertising Literacy Mediate the Effects of Advertising on Children? A Critical Examination of Two Linked Research Literatures in Relation to Obesity and Food Choice." *Journal of Communication* 56 (2006): 560–84. *Academic Search Premier*. EBSCOhost. Denison University, Granville, OH. 6 August 2006 <http://search.epnet.com>.

Don't despair if at first all of these rules seem complicated. Much of this material is probably review, and all of it will become second nature to you with practice. The procedures for quoting and paraphrasing are vitally important, even if they strike you at first as merely cosmetic or surface details. Following these conventions will reassure your readers that you are ethical, competent, and careful. And if all of the papers you write are put in proper form before you turn them in, you free your professor to comment on the substance of what you say—things that probably both of you find more interesting. After all, your professor has only a limited amount of space and time to devote to commenting on your writing, and if your paper is in poor form, you waste valuable time that could be spent on more interesting matters.

Keep this book and refer to it whenever your memory of these conventions fades. On page 52, I've provided a brief checklist. You should consult it while revising papers that employ quoted or paraphrased material.

# A FURTHER NOTE
# ABOUT STYLE
# MANUALS

U nless you have already chosen a major or a field of specialization, it doesn't make sense for you to purchase the standard style manual for every course you take in different fields. Most writing handbooks include enough information about the major style manuals to suffice in introductory classes. Once you are committed to a field of study, however, it is important for you to purchase the manual that your professor or advisor recommends for that field. You will discover that many of the features of manuscript form, some of the features of writing style, and the formats both for in-text citations and for lists of references at the end of a work differ from one field to the next in significant ways. Learning to apply the guidelines for your field is part of learning the field. It might seem that the differences from one field to the next are tiny, and they might seem arbitrary or merely a matter of a teacher's preference. But the guidelines are not, in fact, arbitrary. They reflect the values and methods of inquiry characteristic of the field to which they apply. For example, when formats in the social sciences seem to emphasize the year of publication, it makes sense because the recentness of information in the natural sciences typically matters more than it might in the humanities. If the social sciences are meticulous about citing all the authors of a multiauthor work, it makes sense because so many research projects involve collaborative or team efforts. You might not always know the reasons for features of the prescribed formats, but your work

~~will appear more mature and professional if you care about and apply the~~
guidelines in the appropriate style manual.

Below are some sample citations, included here only to illustrate a few of
the differences among some prominent styles.

### An article in a weekly magazine

**MLA** (*MLA Handbook for Writers of Research Papers*)
Strouse, Jean. "The Unknown J. P. Morgan." <u>The New Yorker</u> 29 March
  1999: 66–79.

**CMS** (*Chicago Manual of Style*)
Strouse, Jean. "The Unknown J. P. Morgan." *The New Yorker*, March 29,
  1999, 66–79.

**CSE** (*Scientific Style and Format*)
Strouse J. 1999 March 29. The unknown J. P. Morgan. New Yorker:
  66–79.

**APA** (*Publication Manual of the American Psychological Association*)
Strouse, J. (1999, March 29). The Unknown J. P Morgan. *The New
  Yorker*, 66–79.

**APSA** (*Style Manual for Political Science*)
Strouse, Jean. 1999. "The Unknown J. P. Morgan." *The New Yorker*,
  March 29: 66–79.

### A book

**MLA**
Glassner, Barry. <u>The Culture of Fear: Why Americans Are Afraid of the
  Wrong Things</u>. New York: Basic Books, 1999.

**CMS**
Glassner, Barry. *The Culture of Fear: Why Americans Are Afraid of the
  Wrong Things*. New York: Basic Books, 1999.

**CSE**
Glassner B. 1999. The culture of fear: why Americans are afraid of the
  wrong things. New York: Basic Books. 276 p.

## APA

Glassner, B. (1999). *The Culture of Fear: Why Americans Are Afraid of the Wrong Things*. New York: Basic Books.

## APSA

Glassner, Barry. 1999. *The Culture of Fear: Why Americans Are Afraid of the Wrong Things*. New York: Basic Books.

## A website

## MLA

Sierra Club. Home page. 2006. Sierra Club. 2 August 2006 <http://www.sierraclub.org/>.

## CMS

Sierra Club. Sierra Club home page. 2006. http://www.sierraclub.org/ (August 2, 2006).

## CSE

Sierra Club. 2006. Sierra Club home page. <http://www.sierraclub.org/>. Accessed 2006 Aug. 2.

## APA

Sierra Club. (2006). Sierra Club home page. Retrieved August 2, 2006, from http://www.sierraclub.org/.

## APSA

Sierra Club. 2006. Sierra Club Home Page. http://www.sierraclub.org/ (accessed Aug. 2, 2006).

# REVISION CHECKLIST FOR QUOTING AND PARAPHRASING

1. Are all of your paragraphs developed adequately, with evidence for your argument or illustration of your complex ideas? Is the paragraph primarily your words, with quotations or paraphrased evidence serving only as supporting material? Do you provide too much information from sources, or too little?
2. If you have paraphrased, did you introduce the material from your source to indicate clearly what is from the source? Did you mention the author? Did you provide a note or a parenthetical citation of the source so that your readers would have all the information they need to locate the source and page from which the information comes?
3. Is the wording of paraphrased material entirely your own? Does it accurately reflect the viewpoint expressed in the original?
4. If you quote, have you introduced each passage, or does your context make it clear that the words are quoted from a source? Have you followed the quotation with a page number or with a note? Is each quoted passage introduced sufficiently so that quoted words fit together grammatically with your own, to assure that your reader will understand the significance of the passage?
5. Are quoted words in proper form? Are they quoted accurately and marked by quotation marks? Have any added words or letters been placed in square brackets, and have deleted words been replaced by an

ellipsis? Have you indicated the line breaks in quoted poetry with slash marks? Have you punctuated the quotations properly?

6. Have you followed all quotations, particularly longer, block quotations, with your own analysis or interpretation of the passages? Are the transitions to and from quoted material smooth and coherent?

7. In your citations of websites, have you made certain that the URL is typed correctly and provided the date that you consulted the source?

8. If you've consulted sources that have been indexed and re-presented by an online database, have you noted the online version that you have cited?

9. Have you followed the format for citations required by the style manual that is used in your discipline? Do all of your citations present all of the necessary information about the works you consulted?

# APPENDIX:
# INTERNET RESOURCES

This section presents useful websites organized by disciplines within the humanities and social sciences. Some of these sites provide resources for research within a discipline, and some provide guides for writing papers and citing sources. Each discipline has its own resources and its own rules, so these sites provide an introduction to these resources and rules. They barely scratch the surface of what's available on the Internet, but they should provide a good start.

## ANTHROPOLOGY

**American Anthropological Association Resources on the Internet**
AAA's list of links of interest to anthropologists.
   http://www.aaanet.org/resinet.htm

**Anthropology in the News**
Contains the latest findings throughout anthropology. Maintained by Texas A&M University.
   http://www.tamu.edu/anthropology/news.html

**Society of American Archaeology Links**
This site has a list of references for archaeologists and archaeology students.
   http://saa.org/links.html

## Voice of the Shuttle: Anthropology and Archaeology Pages

These sites have references to a wide range of current writings from anthropologists and archaeologists, as well as general resources.
http://vos.ucsb.edu

## WWW Virtual Library: Anthropology

General anthropology resource with links for each subdiscipline within
anthropology.
http://vlib.anthrotech.com

# COMMUNICATION

## EraM—Ethnicity, Racism, and Media Discussion Forum

This site explores the issues surrounding ethnicity, racism, and the media.
http://www.blackagenda.com/cybercolonies/eram/index.htm

## Handouts and Links: Communications

Describes steps for planning and writing papers in communications studies
courses, with links to other writing resources, at The Writing Center, University of North Carolina, Chapel Hill.
http://www.unc.edu/depts/wcweb/handouts/communications.html

## National Speakers Association

Resources for speakers, whether professional or amateur.
http://www.nsaspeaker.org

## Online Communication Studies Resources

This site contains an index of online resources for communication studies, including advertising, film studies, and political communication. Maintained
by the Department of Communication Studies at the University of Iowa.
http://www.uiowa.edu/~commstud/resources

## Political Communication Resources

A gateway to Internet sites containing useful information about the media
and democracy.
http://depts.washington.edu/bennett/

## Toastmasters International

Tips for making speeches put together by Toastmasters International.
http://www.toastmasters.org/pdfs/top10.pdf

Voice of the Shuttle: Media Studies Page
This site has references to a wide range of current writings from media studies scholars, as well as general resources.
http://vos.ucsb.edu


## ENGLISH AND COMPOSITION

### Elements of Style
The online version of the popular English composition handbook.
http://www.bartleby.com/141

### EServer Rhetoric and Composition
Links to resources in rhetoric and composition.
http://www.rhetoric.eserver.org

### Literature and Composition Resources
Maintained by Frostburg State University, a guide to quality resources, both primary and secondary, on the Web.
http://faculty.frostburg.edu/engl/gartner/Litcomp.htm

### Modern Language Association
Official website of the MLA. Includes a section on frequently asked questions about MLA style as well as links to resources and publications.
http://www.mla.org

### The OWL at Purdue
An online writing lab offering free writing help and teaching resources. Maintained by Purdue University.
http://owl.english.purdue.edu

### Resources for Writers and Writing Instructors
Links to a number of writing resources, maintained by Jack Lynch at Rutgers University.
http://andromeda.rutgers.edu/~jlynch/Writing/links.html

### Writing@CSU
"Home of Colorado State University's online learning environment, the Writing Studio. Use this site to learn to write, save your work in a private password-protected account, and get feedback on your writing."
http://writing.colostate.edu

## FILM STUDIES

### American Film Institute
AFI is a national institute providing leadership in screen education.
http://www.afi.com

### Dartmouth Writing Program
Features tips for writing about film.
http://www.dartmouth.edu/~writing/materials/student/humanities/
film.shtml

### George Mason University Writing Center Guide to Writing about Film
This useful guide for film writing includes questions to consider when writing
about film and cinematic elements to "read." Contains useful resources.
http://www.gmu.edu/departments/writingcenter/handouts/film.html

### IFILM
A film portal and directory with editorial information and links to over 5,000
domestic and foreign Internet films.
http://www.ifilm.com

### The Internet Movie Database
An award-winning movie website that includes reviews of current movies,
message boards, and a vast database of films.
http://www.imdb.com

### Movie Review Query Engine
A guide to film reviews.
http://www.mrqe.com

### Sandhills Community College
Guidelines for writing about film.
http://www.sandhills.cc.nc.us/english/shared/160guidelines.html

## GEOGRAPHY

### About Geography
A list of current articles on geography in the news, as well as general resources.
http://geography.about.com

**Internet Resources for Geographers**

General resources for geography. Maintained by the Department of Geography at the University of Colorado, Boulder.

http://www.colorado.edu/geography/virtdept/resources/contents.htm

**Internet Resources for Geography and Geology**

General resources for geography and geology. Maintained by the University of Wisconsin, Stevens Point.

http://www.uwsp.edu/geo/internet/geog_geol_resources.html

**Map Projections Poster**

Map projections resources maintained by the U.S. Geological Survey.

http://mac.usgs.gov/mac/isb/pubs/MapProjections/projections.html

**Maps and Cartography**

Earth Science and Map Library Map Collection at the University of California, Berkeley.

http://www.lib.berkeley.edu/EART/MapCollections.html

**New Books in Geography**

A list of new books in geography. Maintained by the Association of American Geographers.

http://www.aag.org/nbig/index.cfm


## HISTORY

**Dartmouth Writing Program**

A student guide to writing a history paper, provided by Dartmouth College.

http://www.dartmouth.edu/~writing/materials/student/soc_sciences/history.shtml

**History**

General resources for history organized by historical time period.

http://www.scholiast.org/history

**History Matters**

History Matters serves as a gateway to Web resources and offers other useful materials for teaching U.S. history.

http://historymatters.gmu.edu

### History Writing Guides

Guide to reading and interpreting primary sources. Very helpful for researchers.
http://academic.bowdoin.edu/WritingGuides

### History and Theory

This website and online journal is devoted to exploring the links between philosophy and history.
http://www.historyandtheory.org

### Voice of the Shuttle: History Page

This site has references to a wide range of writings from world historians, as well as general resources.
http://vos.ucsb.edu

### Women's Biographies: Distinguished Women of Past and Present

This site is devoted to the history of women throughout the world.
http://www.DistinguishedWomen.com

### World History Matters

World History Matters is a portal to world history links on the Web.
http://worldhistorymatters.org

### WWW VL The World Wide Web Virtual Library: History Index

General resource with links to many history resources. Maintained by the University of Kansas.
http://vlib.iue.it/history

## JOURNALISM

### The Associated Press Style Book

An important style guide for all popular publications. People who do public relations and advertising generally follow AP style as well in their writing. It is also a good guide for general writing.
http://www.apstylebook.com

### Association for Education in Journalism and Mass Communication Links

A list of links to appropriate, noncommercial websites of interest to members of the Association for Education in Journalism and Mass Communication.
http://www.aejmc.org/links

**JournalismNet**

JournalismNet is an extensive list of resources for journalists, including daily news updates.

http://www.journalismnet.com

**The Journalist's Toolbox**

The Journalist's Toolbox contains links to areas of interest to journalists, as well as teaching tools for editors and professors. Maintained by the American Press Institute.

http://www.americanpressinstitute.org/pages/toolbox

**The Poynter Center**

A resource for writing about news and current affairs.

http://poynter.org

**Project for Excellence in Journalism: Understanding News in the Information Age**

The website of the Project for Excellence in Journalism, a research organization that specializes in using empirical methods to evaluate and study the performance of the press. Features news and links to other resources.

http://www.journalism.org

**Robert Niles Journalism Help**

Basic statistics for journalists or other laypersons.

http://www.robertniles.com

**Society of Professional Journalists**

The website of the Society of Professional Journalists, a large and broad-based, national journalism organization.

http://www.spj.org


## PHILOSOPHY

**The American Philosophical Association's Web Resources**

A list of philosophical associations and societies, centers and institutes, and electronic texts. Maintained by the American Philosophical Association.

http://www.apa.udel.edu/apa/resources

## Dartmouth Writing Program

A student guide to writing a philosophy paper, provided by Dartmouth College.

http://www.dartmouth.edu/~writing/materials/student/humanities/philosophy.shtml

## Descartes' Meditations Home Page

This site contains an online edition of Descartes' classic work of philosophical reflections.

http://www.wright.edu/cola/descartes

## Ethics Updates Home Page

This site contains resources on the following topics: moral theory, relativism, pluralism, religion, and egoism.

http://ethics.acusd.edu/

## Philosophers: Main Page

This site provides easy access to resources in philosophy, categorized by philosopher.

http://www.epistemelinks.com/Main/MainPers.asp

## Philosophy Comix

This site contains examples of philosophical topics from contemporary comic strips.

http://members.aol.com/lshauser/phlcomix.html

## Philosophy News Service

A list of contemporary news in philosophy.

http://www.philosophynews.com/PNS

## Philosophy Pages

This site focuses on Web links to Western philosophy sites.

http://www.philosophypages.com/index.htm

## Philosophy, Introduction

This site provides a general overview of what philosophy is.

http://pespmc1.vub.ac.be/PHILOSI.html

## Stanford Encyclopedia of Philosophy

An extensive online encyclopedia of philosophy.

http://plato.stanford.edu

Voice of the Shuttle: Philosophy Page
This site has references to a wide range of writings from philosophers, as well
as general resources.
http://vos.ucsb.edu

## POLITICAL SCIENCE

**Inter-university Consortium for Political and Social Research Front Page**
This site contains social science data and resources for researchers.
http://www.icpsr.umich.edu/

**Resources for Political Science**
A list of political science organizations, research in progress, and upcoming
publications. Maintained by the American Political Science Association.
http://apsanet.org/section_188.cfm

**Voice of the Shuttle: Politics and Government Page**
This site has references to a wide range of writings from scholars of politics
and government, as well as general resources.
http://vos.ucsb.edu

**WWW Resources for Political Scientists**
This site contains links to political science resources organized by topic and
type of resource. Maintained by the University of Colorado, Boulder.
http://osiris.colorado.edu/POLSCI/links.html

## RELIGION

**AAR Other Resources**
The American Academy of Religion's list of other resources for religious
studies scholars.
http://www.aarweb.org/other/default.asp

**Dartmouth Writing Program**
A student guide to writing a religion paper, provided by Dartmouth College.
http://www.dartmouth.edu/~writing/materials/student/humanities/
religion.shtml

**Voice of the Shuttle: Religious Studies Page**
This site has references to a wide range of general religious studies resources, as well as links to sites dedicated to the thinkings of many major religious and spiritual groups.
http://vos.ucsb.edu


## SOCIOLOGY

**American Sociological Association Manuscript Checklist**
http://asanet.org/pubs/notice.pdf

**Classical Sociological Theory**
This site contains online texts of classical social thinkers. Maintained by the University of Chicago.
http://www.spc.uchicago.edu/ssr1/PRELIMS/theory.html

**Dartmouth Writing Program**
A student guide to writing a sociology paper, provided by Dartmouth College.
http://www.dartmouth.edu/~writing/materials/student/soc_sciences/sociology.shtml

**Online Communication Studies Resources**
This site contains an index of online resources for cultural studies. Maintained by the Department of Communication Studies at the University of Iowa.
http://www.uiowa.edu/~commstud/resources

**Social Science Hub**
Excellent starting point for research. Comprehensive enough to include many of the major categories within the discipline.
http://www.sshub.com/

**SociologyOnline**
This British site for all students of sociology, criminology, and social thought is full of information about both classical and contemporary thinkers.
http://www.sociologyonline.co.uk/

**SocioSite**

This site, maintained by the University of Amsterdam, provides a global per-
spective on sociology with access to a number of European theorists.
http://www.sociosite.net/index.php

**Voice of the Shuttle: Cultural Studies Page**

This site has references to a wide range of current sociological thinkers, many
specifically oriented toward cultural theories.
http://vos.ucsb.edu